Pokémon™

POCKET EXPERT

Written by Glenn Dakin

CONTENTS

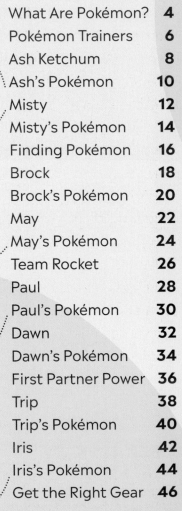

ABOUT THIS BOOK

Welcome to the world of Pokémon—a place of talented Trainers, cool creatures, and epic battles! In this handy guide, you'll find exciting facts and stats on Pokémon and get the lowdown on cool Trainers, like Ash. Then test your skills with an awesome quiz on page 76.

Get ready to become a **Pokémon expert**!

WHAT ARE POKÉMON?

Pokémon are creatures of all shapes and sizes, each with their own special abilities. They live happily in the wild—but can form a deep bond with a human Trainer and become a friend for life!

MANY TYPES

These creatures come in an incredible variety of types. You can find Electric, Grass, even Ghost-types!

Ghost-type, Gengar

TALK THE TALK

Pokémon can communicate with each other, but very few can speak to humans. It takes a long time for Trainers to build up a rapport with their partner.

Ash has a very strong friendship with Pikachu

TIME FOR A CHANGE

Most Pokémon don't stay in the same form for all their lives but change into completely new forms. This ability is called Evolution.

Tsareena

A cute little Bounsweet evolves into an elegant Tsareena!

Bounsweet

BATTLE READY

It is a curious fact that Pokémon love to battle! Some enjoy it as a sport, while others see it as a chance to unlock new abilities.

Four-armed fighter, Machamp

THEIR WORLD

Pokémon live in a world divided into many beautiful and diverse regions. Some Pokémon can be found almost everywhere, like Butterfree. Others are incredibly rare, like the elusive Mew.

Mew

ROTOM DATA

Pokémon are not permanently harmed in battle—they only tire.

POKÉMON TRAINERS

There are many different kinds of Trainers. Most train Pokémon for battle, at special Gyms. Others prepare to perform in Pokémon Showcases or in unique sports. Every Trainer's path calls for dedication and a love of Pokémon.

TRAINER SECRETS

What makes a good Trainer? There is no one way to succeed—every Trainer follows their own path—but it is vital to build a bond of trust with your Pokémon. The closer you are, the more unbeatable you become!

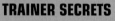

A hug shows the affection between Goh and Cinderace.

GOOD VS. BAD

Can you get bad Pokémon Trainers? Well, there are some, like Paul, who do not care about the feelings of their Pokémon. It's up to Trainers, like Ash, to show that a warm heart and friendly approach get better results.

Paul

UNIQUE BOND

Every Trainer connects with their Pokémon in a different way. Sensitive Lillie was afraid of Pokémon until she was given an egg to look after. It brought out her protective side and she bonded with her Vulpix, Snowy, when it hatched.

Lillie and Snowy

SUPER STADIUMS

A bonus of becoming a top Trainer is the amazing places you get to battle. Ash competed at the super-cool Manalo Stadium in the Alola region.

Ash and Pikachu get ready for the Battle Royal 151.

TOP TOURNAMENTS

The biggest contest, the World Coronation Series, is open to all Trainers. Anyone can enter and compete to rise up the rankings, hoping to make the elite Masters Eight, or even be crowned Monarch.

Visquez hosts a Coronation Series battle at the Vermilion Gym.

ROTOM DATA

A Trainer can begin their Pokémon journey at the young age of 10.

ASH KETCHUM

With a big heart and big dreams, Ash only ever had one desire—to become a Pokémon Master. With his Pokémon pal Pikachu by his side, he eventually fulfilled his wish and won the World Coronation Series.

> "My Pokémon team is faster than light!"

FLYING FRIENDS

Some Trainers specialize in one type of Pokémon, but Ash loves to work with all kinds. In the Kalos region, he trained this flying team of Fletchinder, Noibat, and Hawlucha to compete in the sky relay race.

Tail shaped like a lightning bolt

Pikachu

Cheeks release energy when Pikachu is angry

KEY FACTS

Height:	1' 4"
Weight:	13.2 lb
Type:	Electric
Category:	Mouse
Weakness:	Ground

MEET THE TRAINER

From Pallet Town in the Kanto region, Ash loves a challenge and quickly learns from any mistake he makes. Loyal and lots of fun—he always finds friends wherever he goes.

Poké Ball used to catch and carry Pokémon

Ash sometimes carries Pikachu in his backpack

Black sneakers with blue highlights

Z-RING POWER

Ash is an expert at mastering the different skills needed in every region. In the Alola region, he earns a Z-Ring, enabling Pikachu to perform epic Z-Moves like Gigavolt Havoc.

ASH'S POKÉMON

Greninja

This stealthy fighter has the remarkable ability to create throwing stars out of compressed water. When hurled with force, they can even shatter metal. Ash first met this Pokémon when it was a young Froakie.

IN SYNC

Greninja enjoys a special bond with Ash and can attain a rare form, Ash-Greninja, in which it is in perfect sync with him. The two perfected this form while rescuing some Spewpa from a blizzard in a forest.

KEY FACTS

Height: 4' 11"
Weight: 88.2 lb
Type: Water-Dark
Category: Ninja
Weakness: Grass, Electric, Fighting, Bug, and Fairy

Webbed hands

Long tongue, worn like a scarf

Splayed feet

Squirtle

Known for looking cool in its stylish sunglasses, Ash's Squirtle was by his side on many travels. If threatened, it retracts its limbs into its shell to unleash a huge squirt of water.

KEY FACTS

Height:	1' 8"
Weight:	19.8 lb
Type:	Water
Category:	Tiny Turtle
Weakness:	Grass and Electric

Tough shell

Wide mouth

Bulbous tail

THE SQUIRTLE SQUAD

Before Ash trained Squirtle, it was the leader of a pack of trouble-making Squirtle in the Kanto region. Officer Jenny trained the crew to become firefighters. They became so famous Team Rocket sold Squirtle Squad merchandise!

MISTY

Misty's a great pal of Ash, and along with Brock they enjoy many travels together. Sparky, emotional, and outspoken, she can appear fearless—when she's not trembling at the sight of a bug!

Staryu

Central red gem

Brown "legs"

KEY FACTS

Height:	2' 7"
Weight:	76.1 lb
Type:	Water
Category:	Star Shape
Weakness:	Grass and Electric

BIKE BUDDIES

Misty first met Ash when he took her bike to rush his injured Pikachu to the Pokémon Center for treatment. Later, Pikachu burned her bike to a crisp. Ash long thought Misty stayed with him only because she was hoping to get a new bike!

Side ponytail

Red suspenders

Denim shorts

MEET THE TRAINER

Misty left her hometown to seek her destiny as an expert in Water-type Pokémon. Although tough on the outside, she's also known for being sensitive and soft-hearted.

"Bugs get me all bugged out!"

SISTER ACT

When Misty's sisters formed a synchronized swimming act called The Three Sensational Sisters, they left Misty out! But sibling rivalry only spurred Misty on. She eventually proved her worth, becoming Cerulean Gym Leader.

MISTY'S POKÉMON

Corsola

A great fighter, Corsola was often Misty's Pokémon of choice in battle, using moves like Spike Cannon. Its coral horns can also trap an opponent. Found in the clean seas of the south, Corsola shuns polluted waters.

KEY FACTS

Height:	2'
Weight:	11 lb
Type:	Water-Rock
Category:	Coral
Weakness:	Grass, Electric, Fighting, and Ground

Central horn

Pink branches

Cute smile

Light blue underbelly

REEF ENCOUNTER

A hyperactive Pokémon, Misty's Corsola caused chaos on Yellow Rock Isle, disturbing others of its kind. Its antics helped prevent Team Rocket from stealing coral, and Misty added it to her team.

Psyduck

Always troubled by a headache, Psyduck is a personality-filled Pokémon with awesome psychic powers. A loose cannon, Psyduck doesn't like staying in its Pokéball and pops up at unlikely moments!

Three black hairs

Hands on head, due to headache

Tiny pupils

Flat cream-colored bill

KEY FACTS

Height:	2' 7"
Weight:	43.2 lb
Type:	Water
Category:	Duck
Weakness:	Grass and Electric

DUCK LUCK

There was a surprise in store for Water-type specialist, Misty, when Brock tried to hand her a Psyduck. She accidentally tripped and dropped a Pokéball—Psyduck pecked at it and ended up inside!

FINDING POKÉMON

Want to catch yourself a Pokémon?
You've got to know where to look! They
can be found almost anywhere across
the known regions of the Pokémon
world, but most live in the wild.

FORESTS

You might find Pokémon
such as Bewear, stufful,
or Mimikyu in the
Ancient Melemele
Forest.

Mimikyu lives
under a cloth that
looks like Pikachu

ICY ISLANDS

Icy places can be
a challenge for
humans, but many
Pokémon enjoy the
wintry weather.

The ice on Eiscue's
head has a salty taste

CAVES

Dark caves are home to
Pokémon like Woobat, which
use their noses to grip onto
the walls as they sleep.

Woobat have
one heart-shaped
nostril

Butterfree are often found in
tropical forests and jungles

SEAS

To see Pokémon that live in
the ocean, like Bruxish and
Sharpedo, explore by
swimming, snorkeling,
or submarine.

Explore the seas off
the Muraille coast

FIELDS

Pokémon sometimes enjoy
hiding in tall grass, or like
Combee, visit flower fields
to gather nectar.

Combee sleep in groups
of about a hundred

LAKES, RIVERS, AND PONDS

Many Pokémon live in the water
or around the water's edge.
These Wooper love a cold
water pond.

Wooper Pond Preschool

BROCK

Dependable Brock comes from a big family with nine younger siblings. He grew up shouldering many duties and became a rock for all to rely on. His only weakness is falling in love with any girl he meets!

TRAVELS WITH ASH

With his father often away, Brock had almost given up on his own dreams of traveling. But a chance meeting with Ash inspired his father to return home—freeing Brock to see the world.

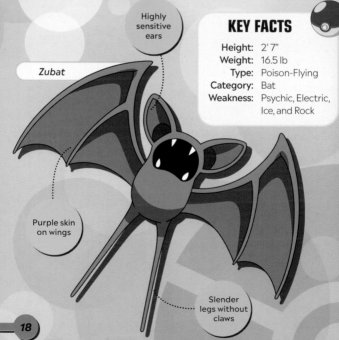

Highly sensitive ears

Zubat

Purple skin on wings

Slender legs without claws

KEY FACTS

Height: 2' 7"
Weight: 16.5 lb
Type: Poison-Flying
Category: Bat
Weakness: Psychic, Electric, Ice, and Rock

MEET THE TRAINER

It's not all about winning battles—Brock believes it's more important to show kindness to all Pokémon. Specializing in Rock-types, his absolute dream is to become a respected Pokémon breeder.

Spiky hair

Green vest

"I'm not called Brock the Rock for nothing, you know!"

Belt with pockets

BROCK AND ROLL

Brock showed just how strong he was when he took on Kiawe. Using a Mega-Evolved Steelix, he smashed Kiawe's Turtonator, exclaiming he was not called "Brock the Rock" for nothing!

BROCK'S POKÉMON

Onix

Always strong in battle, this serpentine Rock-type has the sheer size to intimidate any opponent—and can evolve to be the even bigger Steelix. It's said to enjoy being polished by its Trainer.

KEY FACTS

Height:	28'10"
Weight:	463 lb
Type:	Rock -Ground
Category:	Rock Snake
Weakness:	Steel, Fighting, Water, Ice, Grass, and Ground

Single horn

White eyes with small pupils

Body made of boulders

THE HARDER THEY FALL...

Onix was Brock's go-to Pokémon for facing challengers at Pewter Gym. It looked so imposing that Pikachu tried to sneak off and avoid the fight! But when their battle set off water sprinklers, it became vulnerable to Electric attacks and was beaten.

Croagunk

This punchy Pokémon unsettles its opponent by filling the air with a weird sound. From its inflated poison sacs, it then delivers a powerful Poison Jab. Brock's Croagunk had the habit of knocking him out to stop him from chasing pretty girls!

KEY FACTS

Height: 2' 4"
Weight: 50.7 lb
Type: Poison-Fighting
Category: Toxic Mouth
Weakness: Psychic, Flying, and Ground

GYM JABBER

When Team Rocket set up a fake Gym to try and steal Pokémon, Croagunk became Jessie's top fighter, beating many challengers with his famous jab. But when their sneaky plan failed, Brock took pity on Croagunk and invited him into his team.

Inflatable cheek pouches

Cunning smile

White bands around midriff

MAY

From the Hoenn region, May is a soft-hearted and easy-going city girl, who loves discovering new shops and foods. She has little interest in battling with Pokémon and mainly travels to see the world.

"I like it... I choose Torchic"

SIBLING DUTIES... TO THE MAX!

One key job that May has is keeping her little brother Max out of trouble. Max is fun—and cheeky. When he met Ash, he pretended to be the Hoenn Gym Leader! Handily Max is also something of a walking Pokédex.

Large crest

Torchic

Stubby beak

KEY FACTS

Height: 1' 4"
Weight: 5.5 lb
Type: Fire
Category: Chick
Weakness: Water, Ground, and Rock

Yellow unformed wings

MEET THE TRAINER

May's main interest is in being a fantastic Pokémon Coordinator. She just loves to bring out the very best in all her Pokémon and to help them win contests. She's trained a wide variety from Eevee to Munchlax.

Red and white headband

Orange belt bag

MAKING IT HAPPEN

May didn't start out as a Coordinator, but she was inspired to follow this path by a cool Coordinator named Janet, who let May and Max join in with her Beautifly performance. The thrill of the contest had May instantly hooked.

Sneakers with white strap

Skitty

This affectionate bundle of energy simply cannot keep still! Skitty can't resist chasing any moving object it sees. It will happily pursue its own tail, running around and around until it gets too dizzy to continue!

Little cream-colored balls

Pink tufts

Sweet smile

Pink pouch

KEY FACTS

Height: 2'
Weight: 24.3 lb
Type: Normal
Category: Kitten
Weakness: Fighting

ASSIST ACTION

Skitty has a special move that comes in very handy in battle. It can surprise an opponent with its Assist Move—taking a move from any other Pokémon in its own team! In Mauville City, it used Torchic's Quick Attack to defeat Watt's Amphoras.

Bulbasaur

May's Bulbasaur has a gentle nature and loves picking flowers. From the day it is born, this Pokémon has a plant seed on its back, which slowly grows throughout its life. It later evolves into Ivysaur and then the powerful Venusaur.

KEY FACTS

Height: 2' 4"
Weight: 15.2 lb
Type:: Grass Poison
Category: Seed
Weakness: Fire, Psychic, Flying, and Ice

Bulb on back

Big red eyes

Dark green markings

Clawed feet

ONE GOOD TURN...

When May first met her Bulbasaur, she saved it from falling off a ledge while it was picking flowers. Later, the Pokémon repaid the help, when along with its Venusaur parent, it saved May and her friends from angry Grass Pokémon in the Forbidden Forest.

TEAM ROCKET

Prepare for trouble and make it double! Not all Trainers have the best of intentions—Team Rocket likes to steal others' Pokémon to form an unbeatable force. Somehow, it never seems to work out that way...

MEOWTH

Team Rocket's Meowth Pokémon is unique in that it walks upright on two legs, like a human, and can actually talk to people!

KEY FACTS

Height: 1' 4"
Weight: 9.3 lb
Type: Normal
Category: Scratch Cat
Weakness: Fighting

Three sharp claws

WOBBUFFET

This loyal Pokémon has traveled with team Rocket for many years. An expert in counterattack, it Inflates its body to strike back at its foe.

KEY FACTS

Height: 4' 3"
Weight: 62.8 lb
Type: Psychic
Category: Patient
Weakness: Ghost, Dark, and Bug

Flat arms

JESSIE

A cool customer who delights in using her acting skills to fool others. She has a talent for training Pokémon—and for getting James to do most of the hard work!

Black thigh boots

JAMES

Like Jessie, James is a little too soft-hearted to make a real villain. He's a caring Trainer who loves his Pokémon. He also loves calling Ash a "twerp"!

Pants tucked into boots

PAUL

With a cool, confident style, Paul is a cold-hearted Trainer who doesn't care what happens to his Pokémon—as long as they win. He also enjoys teasing his opponents!

Leaf absorbs solar power

Turtwig

Shell of hardened soil

BIG BROTHER IS WATCHING...

Paul is inspired by his big brother, Reggie, who's also a Pokémon Trainer. When Paul suffers a total six-zero defeat to Brandon in the Battle Pyramid, Reggie shows compassion and tells him not to be guided by negative emotions.

KEY FACTS

Height:	1' 04"
Weight:	22.5 lbs
Type:	Grass
Category:	Tiny Leaf
Weakness:	Fire, Flying, Ice, Poison, and Bug

RUTHLESS STYLE

In his first encounter with Ash, Paul scanned his three Starly to see which one knew the Aerial Ace move. He then coldly rejected the other two, which made Ash mad—and so the pair became rivals.

MEET THE TRAINER

Paul won't spend hours improving a Pokémon's skills and beliefs—he scans them with his Pokédex and only keeps the most powerful. He thinks anything else is a waste of time.

Zip-up jacket

Shaggy hairstyle

"Take a hike! I don't need you!"

Purple sneakers with white soles

PAUL'S POKÉMON

Torterra

This Pokémon is so immense it has a tree growing from its back. In ancient times, people believed that an absolutely gigantic Torterra could be found somewhere beneath the earth. It begins life as the gentler Turtwig.

KEY FACTS

Height: 7' 3"
Weight: 683.4 lb
Type: Grass-Ground
Category: Continent
Weakness: Fire, Flying, Bug, and Ice

Living tree

Ridge of spikes

Armored shell

Head spikes

TOUGH TEAMMATE

Hard to damage, Torterra is useful for draining an opponent's strength. It was unhurt by Ash's Chimchar's fierce Flamethrower, forcing Ash to rethink his strategy.

Electivire

Excitement drives on this feisty fighter, as the rate of its pulse increases its electrical energy. In a battle situation, this results in a high voltage power surge, and often victory.

A CLOSER BOND

At the Lily of the Valley Conference battle, Electivire was beaten by Ash's Infernape. Instead of getting mad, Paul thanked his Pokémon for a good battle—a sign of a growing respect.

KEY FACTS

Height: 5' 11"
Weight: 305.6 lb
Type: Electric
Category: Thunderbolt
Weakness: Ground

Round antennae

One of two black tails

Furry mane

Human-like hands

DAWN

Level-headed and good at asking the right questions, Dawn isn't easily fooled. She's bright, optimistic, and cheerfully bounces back from any setback. Dressing up is also very important to her—she has a flair for looking good at all times.

SECRET NAME

At school, Dawn was once given an electric shock by Plusle and Minun. They covered her hair with sparks that one joker said looked like "diamond dandruff." This is how she got the nickname Dee-Dee, although she doesn't like admitting this!

Three blue spikes

Yellow cheeks store electricity

Large tail

Pachirisu

KEY FACTS

Height: 1' 4"
Weight: 8.6 lb
Type: Electric
Category: EleSquirrel
Weakness: Ground

MEET THE TRAINER

Eager to follow in her mother's footsteps, Dawn wants to be a top Pokémon Coordinator. She treasures the first prize ribbon her mother ever won, and carries it with her as a good-luck charm.

White beanie hat

Red scarf

"No need to worry!"

Pokétch watch

BOUNCING BACK

Discouraged by early failures, Dawn bravely took part in the Floaroma Town Contest for Pokémon Coordinators. It was the battle of the Piplup, as Dawn narrowly beat her old school rival, Kenny, to the prize. Afterward, she called her mom to share the news!

DAWN'S POKÉMON

Piplup

A proud Pokémon, Piplup is a free spirit who does not like taking orders. It also doesn't want to be looked after, so can be generally hard to bond with. One of its top moves is Bubble Beam—opening its beak to unleash a bubbly bombardment!

KEY FACTS

Height: 1' 4"
Weight: 11.5 lb
Type: Water
Category: Penguin
Weakness: Grass and Electric

Crown shape above beak

Dark blue tail

Flipper arms

White dots on chest

PENGUIN PAL

Piplup and Dawn did not get off to a good start. When Dawn tried to catch it, Piplup fired Bubble Beam at her! They finally bonded when they had to join forces to escape a horde of angry Ariados—and have stayed pals ever after.

Mamoswine

Hard to impress, it can often take Mamoswine a while to warm to its Trainer. Some even fall asleep when given orders! This heavy-hitter has been around for ages—it's shown in wall paintings from 10,000 years ago. For a while, it was believed to be extinct.

KEY FACTS

Height: 8' 2"
Weight: 641.5 lb
Type: Ice-Ground
Category: Twin Tusk
Weakness: Steel, Fire, Grass, Water, and Fighting

Blue mask shape around eyes

Large white tusks

Three gray toes

A MAMMOTH BOND

When a Mamoswine was injured by a wild Aggron in Sinnoh Forest, Dawn tended to its wounds, made it a soft bed, and fed it Oran Berries. Her loving care healed Mamoswine and inspired it to later send Team Rocket blasting off.

35

FIRST PARTNER POWER

Every region hands out three different first partner Pokémon. They are all chosen to be ideal for a young Trainer to bond with. That first Pokémon you choose changes your life!

ASH AND PIKACHU

Frankly, Ash really wanted Squirtle, but when he met Pikachu, and received his first electric shock, he knew they were made for each other!

The dream team!

CHLOE AND EEVEE

Chloe Cerise never had her own Pokémon until she saw an Eevee she thought was in peril from two lab workers. Her protective instinct created an instant bond.

Eevee loved Chloe's caring nature from the start.

GUZMA AND GOLISOPOD

Not all first partnerships run smoothly. Guzma likes to blame his Golisopod for failures and aims angry comments at it during a battle. But deep down there is an undying bond.

Guzma

Golisopod

Gary Oak

Squirtle

GARY OAK AND SQUIRTLE

Gary beat Ash to this Pokémon, on their first day as Trainers. Ambitious Gary believed Squirtle to be the best, and the competitive pair were well matched.

SOPHOCLES AND TOGEDEMARU

With his feisty exterior and big heart, Sophocles was a natural pairing with his spiky first partner. Sophocles likes Electric-types, who can help him with his science projects.

This pair are champs at balloon popping contests!

ROTOM DATA

First partners can be handed out by professors, caught in the wild, or received as family gifts.

TRIP

Loner Trip has no time for making friends, and it can be tough just persuading him you are even worth battling! A keen photographer, he's likely to be found snapping new Pokémon... and plenty of selfies too!

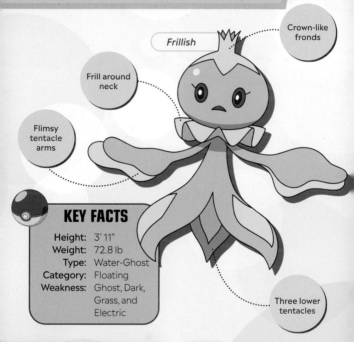

Frillish

Crown-like fronds

Frill around neck

Flimsy tentacle arms

Three lower tentacles

KEY FACTS

Height: 3' 11"
Weight: 72.8 lb
Type: Water-Ghost
Category: Floating
Weakness: Ghost, Dark, Grass, and Electric

TRIP TRIPS UP

When a Venipede swarm covers Castella City, Trip uses his Lampent to fight their leader. But Local Gym Leader, Burgh, advises not to use aggression. Trip sees his mistake and instead uses Tranquill to help the Venipede leave calmly.

MEET THE TRAINER

Trip's logical approach doesn't allow for the feelings of others. He likes to rile an opponent by telling them they don't know the basics. Despite being a great Trainer, he's often a very bad sport!

Hooded top

ALDER AND WISER

They say never meet your heroes, and Trip might agree after meeting Alder. He'd waited years to battle the hero he met once as a child, but Alder defeated Trip easily in a duel and left him humbled.

Orange jacket

"Let's get this journey started!"

Gray pants

TRIP'S POKÉMON

Snivy

Smart Snivy is a formidable opponent in battle, with attacks like Tackle and Leaf Tornado. Naturally fast, it is even quicker when exposed to sunlight. When grappling its foes, it uses vines more effectively than its hands.

KEY FACTS

Height: 2'
Weight: 17.9 lb
Type: Grass
Category: Grass Snake
Weakness: Fire, Flying, Ice, Poison, and Bug

Large brown eyes

Leaf on tip of tail

Leaflike feet

Serpentine tail

SERPERIOR NO MORE

Right from their first battle, Snivy seemed to have the advantage over Pikachu. Ash met Trip's Pokémon in all its forms, but it was as Serperior that it finally faced defeat, when Pikachu blasted it with Iron Tail and Electro Ball.

Tranquill

This peaceful-looking Pokémon has a few surprises in store, including its dynamic Air Cutter attack. As well as being a fairly quick flyer, Tranquill has a wonderful sense of direction, and it will always find its way home from an adventure.

Red markings above eyes

Tuft of black feathers

KEY FACTS

Height: 2'
Weight: 33.1 lb
Type: Normal-Flying
Category: Wild Pigeon
Weakness: Electric, Ice, and Rock

Frill at back of neck

Pink talons with black tips

FLYING ACE

One of Tranquill's greatest duels took place in Luxuria Town, where Trip beat Ash in battle. Tranquill used Double Team, so Ash's Tepig didn't know which target to hit. Then finished off its Fire-type foe with a shattering Aerial Ace.

IRIS

This spirited Trainer is a natural healer, helping her Pokémon and others by making herbal remedies. A rebel, she ran away from an elite school in Unova to fulfill her dreams.

A SWINGING TIME

Among Iris's surprising skills is a talent for swinging on vines. It's the coolest way to travel in the forests of her home! She even taught Dawn the skill when she was chased by some grouchy Onix.

"I'm no kid! I'm the Champion!"

Strong horn

Sharp tusks, used as knives in ancient times

Axew

Light green collar

KEY FACTS

Height: 2' 0
Weight: 39.7 lb
Type: Dragon
Category: Tusk
Weakness: Fairy, Ice, and Dragon

Coming from the Village of Dragons, Iris is an expert in dragon behavior, earning their trust by understanding their feelings. She teaches that the way to win is to have fun while battling.

Twin pigtails

Golden hair ties

THE DRAGON SQUAD

Iris wanted to battle Ash when she became the strongest Trainer in Unova. She had assembled a powerful Dragon squad, leading off with Dragonite. But dino beat dragon when Ash surprised her with his ancient Fossil Pokémon, Dracovish.

IRIS'S POKÉMON

Excadrill

This tough Pokémon can spin its body like a drill, shaking its opponents off their feet. People often mistake the vast tunnels it creates for natural phenomena. It begins life as the Mole Pokémon, Drilbur.

KEY FACTS

Height: 2' 4"
Weight: 89.1 lb
Type: Ground-Steel
Category: Subterrene
Weakness: Fire, Water, Fighting, and Ground

Ridged head blade

Two red stripes on cheeks

Digging blades instead of claws

Short powerful legs

DIGGING DEEP FOR TRUST

Excadrill once fell out with Iris because she made it use tactics that led to a painful defeat by the Haxorus of Dragon Master, Drayden. Later, she apologized, inspiring Excadrill to bounce back and fight again.

Emolga

A playful Pokémon, Emolga's cute antics can sometimes lead to trouble. It looks harmless as it glides through the air but can deliver a powerful electric shock, like Pikachu. Its Attract move can make foes fall in love with it!

Yellow spots on cheeks

Large rounded ears

Tail for steering in flight

Thin skin for gliding

KEY FACTS

Height: 1' 4"
Weight: 11.0 lb
Type: Electric-Flying
Category: Sky Squirrel
Weakness: Ice and Rock

ROCKING TEAM ROCKET

It once seemed that Emolga had joined Team Rocket. In fact, it was just part of a plan to impress Iris. Emolga used her position inside Team Rocket to protect her true friends—and helped send Jessie and James blasting off, as usual.

GET THE RIGHT GEAR

It takes skill and heart to be a Pokémon Trainer, but you need the right equipment as well. Here are the essential items to get started—every serious Trainer will have them in their backpack.

POKÉDEX

In many regions, from Kanto to Kalos, the Pokédex is your go-to source for Pokémon data, giving a Trainer the lowdown on any Pokémon they discover.

Kanto Pokédex

Standard Poké Ball

Safari Poké Ball

Ultra Poké Ball

POKÉ BALL

You cannot catch a Pokémon without your Poké Ball! They are designed to keep your Pokémon safe until called into action. Special kinds exist from the Safari Ball to Ultra Ball.

ROTOM PHONE

Recently, this handy gadget has taken the role of the Pokédex. When a Rotom Pokémon possesses a phone, it becomes a bright, chatty assistant.

Rotom Dex

POTION

A fast-acting spray that will help an injured Pokémon heal. Always useful in a crisis and helps gain a Pokémon's trust.

Professor Kukui gives Potion to Rockruff.

Z-RING

Z-Ring

In the Alola region, this will allow you to do Z-Moves, making a Trainer become at one with their Pokémon.

DYNAMAX BAND

Vital in Galar region, where local Power Spots enable you to grow your Pokémon to giant size—if you have this band to control it.

Goh was given this Dynamax Band by Sonia, in Galar.

ROTOM DATA

Carrying Pokémon food is a great way to make friends. Pokémon love Sitrus and Pecha Berries!

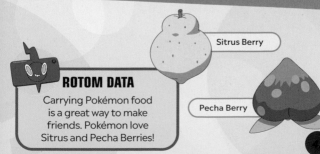

Sitrus Berry

Pecha Berry

CLEMONT

A brilliant mind and a kind heart sum up this Trainer. With a wonderful gift for invention, Clemont is always trying to create devices that help locate, study, and benefit Pokémon in every way.

"The future is now, thanks to science!"

BATTLING BOT

Clemont designed the clever Clembot to run Lumiose Gym in his absence. But when it gave electric shocks to Trainers who had not collected four Gym Badges, he had to reprogram it to be more friendly!

KEY FACTS

Height:	4' 7"
Weight:	92.6 lb
Type:	Electric
Category:	Gleam Eyes
Weakness:	Ground

Spiked black mane

Gold star on tail

Bright golden eyes

Luxray

MEET THE TRAINER

The Leader of Lumiose City Gym, Clemont specializes in Electric-type Pokémon. He believes science has the answer to improving your skills, but Ash has taught him to trust his feelings, too.

Round glasses

MATCHMAKER BONNIE

It's a full-time job for Clemont looking after his kid sister Bonnie. She follows him everywhere, asking every girl they meet if they'd like to marry him. He finds it so embarrassing!

Pockets for tools and gadgets

Light blue lab suit

CLEMONT'S POKÉMON

Chespin

Chespin is a feisty fighter who just loves pastries! Beware those soft quills on its head—they can become so hard and sharp they shatter rock! Its ultimate form is the armored powerhouse, Chesnaught.

Small orange nose

Clawed feet

Chestnut-shell-like head covering

KEY FACTS

Height: 1'4"
Weight: 19.8 lb
Type: Grass
Category: Spiny Nut
Weakness: Fire, Flying, Ice, Poison, and Bug

Orange tip on tail

MACARONS AND MEOWTH

Chespin first appeared when it was seen sneakily scoffing macaroons at Professor Sycamore's lab. It later went on to help beat Team Rocket, by pulling the plug on their Mega Meowth robot.

KEY FACTS

Height: 8"
Weight: 4.9 lb
Type: Electric-Fairy
Category: Antenna
Weakness: Poison and Ground

Dedenne

This mischievous character is happy to steal the snacks of other Pokémon. It uses its tail to absorb electricity from people's homes and charge itself. Clemont's Dedenne has also used its electrical powers to track down Pikachu.

Antenna-like whiskers

Sharp teeth

Short arms with stubby paws

Tail like an electric cord

CRASH LANDING

Dedenne was an immediate hit with Bonnie, especially as it fell out of a tree and landed on her head! As she was too young to catch it, Clemont kindly caught it on her behalf, showing what a cool big brother he is!

SERENA

Bringing fun and energy into the lives of all around her, Serena makes Pokévision videos, designs Pokémon fashions, and is also a top baker specializing in sweet treats like Poké Puffs and macaroons!

Black-ringed eyes

Cream-colored tufts

Green leaf

KEY FACTS

Height: 2'
Weight: 17.6 lb
Type: Fighting
Category: Playful
Weakness: Psychic, Flying, and Fairy

Pancham

RHYHORN REBEL

Life could have been very different for Serena if she'd listened to her mother and become a Rhyhorn Racer. She had no love for the sport and, inspired by Ash, left home for new horizons.

MEET THE TRAINER

Serena is dedicated to competing in Pokémon Showcases—dazzling performances in which Trainer and partner show off their skills. Following this dream requires artistry and resilience.

Dark pink hat

"I am always one with my Pokémon."

SHOWCASE STAR

Serena quickly secured the three Princess Keys she needed to qualify for the contest to become Kalos Queen. Even at this Master Class level, she shone out, but just failed to beat reigning queen, Aria, in the Gloire final.

Pleated skirt with side pocket

Black sneakers with pink design

Sylveon

It has a natural urge to dance when living in the wild—and with training, Sylveon can perform awe-inspiring displays. Gentle and kind, it can use its ribbon-like feelers to send a calming aura to its opponents, and turn anger to peace.

Flowing feelers

Fluffy pink ears

Pale blue eyes

KEY FACTS

Height: 3' 3"
Weight: 51.8 lb
Type: Fairy
Category: Intertwining
Weakness: Steel and Poison

Dainty pink paws

SYLVEON'S EVOLUTION

Fate seemed destined to make Sylveon and Serena partners. As an Eevee, it saved Serena's life when it stopped her from walking over a cliff edge. Impressed with Eevee's talents, Serena put on an outdoor show, which persuaded it to join her.

Braixen

This graceful Pokémon loves to dance but is a fiery fury in battle—creating friction in its fur to set fire to the twig it keeps in its tail. Braixen evolves into future-seeing Fox Pokémon, Delphox.

KEY FACTS

Height: 3' 3"
Weight: 32.0 lb
Type: Fir
Category: Fox
Weakness: Water, Ground, and Rock

Twig that can be set on fire

Orange-tipped tail

White fur collar

Yellow fur "skirt"

BRAIXEN BLAZES BRIGHT

Serena's first partner Pokémon was a Fennekin that evolved into Braixen during a double battle with Aria. It has starred in some of Serena's greatest displays—creating a ring of fire and a flower of fire.

AWESOME EVOLUTIONS

The ability to evolve is one of the most incredible things about Pokémon. Most have three stages, although there are many intriguing exceptions...

NO EVOLUTION

Ditto is an example of no Evolution, but it can make itself look like any other Pokémon!

Ditto

TWO-STAGE EVOLUTION

A surprising example of a two-stage Evolution is Stufful. It looks like a cute teddy bear... until it evolves into the powerful Bewear!

Bewear

Stufful

THREE-STAGE EVOLUTION

Most Pokémon have a three-stage Evolution—like Pichu, that can become Pikachu, then Raichu. Ash's Pikachu, however, has decided not to evolve!

Pikachu

Pichu

EEVEE'S EVOLUTIONS

One of the most amazing Pokémon of all is Eevee. It currently has eight possible Evolutions! These include fiery Flareon, snowy Glaceon, and the Electric-type, Jolteon.

Eevee

Flareon

Vaporeon

Leafeon

Sylveon

Glaceon

Umbreon

Jolteon

Espeon

Raichu

ROTOM DATA

Some Pokémon, like Bulbasaur, evolve in spectacular mass gatherings!

KIAWE

Brave-hearted Kiawe strives to protect his homeland—the volcanic Akala Island. He loves to instruct others in the ways of nature, and working the family farm is just as important to him as studying Pokémon.

TOP FOUR FIGHTER

In the Alola region's big tournament, The Manalo Conference, Kiawe made it to the final four, defeating his friend Sophocles. He was beaten by Gladion in a spectacular semifinal.

Stoutland

KEY FACTS

Height: 3' 11"
Weight: 134.5 lb
Type: Normal
Category: Big-Hearted
Weakness: Fighting

Bulky gray fur

Flowing whiskers

Stout body

MEET THE TRAINER

Kiawe specializes in Fire-types, training at night after all his chores are finished. He studies Z-Moves, believing only those who love all living things should use such power.

ULTRA GUARDIAN

Kiawe is a member of the Ultra Guardians—a team dedicated to saving the Alola region from the mysterious Ultra Beasts that invade the region. Along with his friends, he helped end the threat.

Flame-inspired hairstyle

Necklace with gems and feathers

Z-Ring bracelet

"Alola to new adventure!"

KIAWE'S POKÉMON

Alolan Marowak

A selfish Pokémon, Alolan Marowak is quick to anger and enjoys provoking its own teammates. Extremely brave, it will take on any opponent, armed with its trusty bone.

Bone used as a weapon

Skull helmet

Small horn on tail

Tough light-brown skin

KEY FACTS

Height:	3'3"
Weight:	99.2 lb
Type:	Ground
Category:	Bone Keeper
Weakness:	Water, Grass, and Ice

CROWN CAPER

Alolan Marowak ran away with the Wela Crown, an important artifact, at the annual Fire Festival. The crown boosted Alolan Marowak's power, but Kiawe and Turtonator finally outfought and caught him!

KEY FACTS

Height: 6′ 7″
Weight: 467.4 lb
Type: Fire-Dragon
Category: Blast Turtle
Weakness: Ground, Rock, and Dragon

Turtonator

A tough opponent to crack, Turtonator has explosive substances in the coating of its shell, which will detonate if touched in battle! In the Alola region's Battle Royal wrestling, its big Z-Move is Inferno Overdrive.

Cannon-style snout

Shell helmet

Detonating spines

Star shell markings

FEARLESS FRIEND

Turtonator showed its selfless character when sly tycoon, Viren, tried to bully Kiawe's family. Viren used Electivire against Kiawe's sister, Mimo. Turtonator took the blast itself, to keep Mimo safe.

LANA

A lover of the sea, and of Water-type Pokémon, Lana spends hours at the seaside with her Popplio. An expert at fishing, she loves to study her catch, then set it free. Don't ask her if Ash is her boyfriend—she will only blush!

BE NICE TO SMALL FRY

Lana had no idea that the injured Wishiwashi she rescued was part of the famous, giant Totem Pokémon. Later, when she caught the Totem, the tiny Wishiwashi gave her a crystal for her first Z-Ring.

Long pointed ears

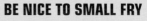
Eevee

Cream-colored mane

Bushy tail

KEY FACTS

Height:	1'
Weight:	14.3 lb
Type:	Normal
Category:	Evolution
Weakness:	Fighting

MEET THE TRAINER

Patient Trainer Lana works hard on the skills of her Popplio, helping it blow bigger water balloons. With her Z-Crystal, she enjoys practicing Water-type Z-Moves like the epic Hydro Vortex.

"I will accept the challenge!"

Swimsuit underneath top

DANGER IN THE DEEP

As Lana and Popplio helped treasure-seeker Kanoa look for a rare jewel, they were attacked by Sea Creeper Pokémon, Dhelmise. Popplio used its Hydro Vortex to help them escape its whirlpool.

Wave motif on pants

LANA'S POKÉMON

Popplio

A friendly Water-type, it inflates water balloons with its nose. A Trainer can use these to ride through the sky or sea. One of Popplio's favorite moves is Bubble Beam, unleashing a bubbly blast against its opponent!

BALLOON POWER

Popplio saved the day when Team Rocket used a big net to scoop up the Ride Pokémon of Lana and her school pals. When Pikachu broke the net, Popplio created a giant water balloon to give them a soft landing.

KEY FACTS

Height:	1' 4"
Weight:	16.5 lb
Type:	Water
Category:	Sea Lion
Weakness:	Grass and Electric

Round pink nose

Pale blue collar

Strong tail

Lapras

Kindly and calm, this majestic mover across the waves loves to carry people and Pokémon on its back. Lapras understands human speech and makes a helpful and considerate friend. Its tough shell protects it in battle.

Spiral ears

Small horn

Thick knobbly shell

Powerful front flippers

KEY FACTS

Height:	8' 2"
Weight:	485 lb
Type:	Water-Ice
Category:	Transport
Weakness:	Grass, Electric, Fighting, and Rock

SMOOTH SAILER

Where would Lana be without her Lapras? This gentle giant takes her on all her marine adventures. She uses it to take Sophocles to see the special sight of a great Wailord rising up out of the water.

POKÉMON SPORTS

Pokémon are not only for battling—
they excel in a wide variety of
unique sports. A good Trainer is
needed too, of course!

POKÉMON SUMO

This earth-shaking sport has
a catch—no Pokémon can use
its moves. In the Harvest Island
contest, Ash's Pignite just uses
its raw power to beat a Golurk
in the big final slam-down.

Pignite

POKÉMON PING PONG

On Melemele Island, Pokémon can use
any moves they like in this cool sport.
Smeargle, the Painter Pokémon, proves
a real artist with the bat and helps
Trainer Ilima to victory.

Smeargle

THE POKÉSLED JUMP TOURNAMENT

On Mount Lanakila, on Ula'ula
Island, amazing feats of sled
jumping can
be seen.
Watch out for
Ninetales,
trained by star
performer, Cerah,
as it has an amazing
Aurora Veil move!

Cerah and Ninetales
demonstrate a basic
Pokésled jump.

Ninetales

EXTREME POKÉMON RACE

Trainers ride skateboards pulled by Pokémon in this race from Johto region. Ash's Bayleef, with its power to pep things up, gave Ash the extra determination to beat his rival Gary.

Ash pipped Gary to the golden Poké Ball prize.

Bayleef

WRESTLING—BATTLE ROYAL STYLE

In the Alola region, wrestling is very popular. Incineroar—the fiery partner of the famous Masked Royal—is the Pokémon to watch!

The human half of this dream team is secretly Ash's Professor Kukui.

Incineroar

ROTOM DATA

Ash and his pals once beat Team Rocket at Pokébase—Pokémon baseball!

GOH

A bright Trainer with an ambitious streak, Goh worked closely with Ash as a research fellow at the Cerise Laboratory. Gentle by nature, he is more interested in discovering Pokémon than dueling.

Cream-colored wings

Scythe-like arms

Scyther

KEY FACTS

Height: 4' 11"
Weight: 123.5 lb
Type: Bug -Flying
Category: Mantis
Weakness: Fire, Flying, Electric, Ice, and Rock

Three sharp claws on feet

GO, GOH!

Goh's greatest moment came when he and Ash helped save the Galar region from the power of the Legendary Pokémon, Eternatus. Goh used the ancient shield and Ash the sword, to become the Galar region's heroes.

MEET THE TRAINER

It is Goh's desire to catch every type of Pokémon. There is no kind he specializes in. Yet despite the size of his growing collection, he will always give special Trainer time to any that need him.

Red highlights in hair

Rotom Phone

"You can count on me!"

Grey hoodie with red trim

CHASING MEW

Goh's aim is to catch Mew—the most elusive Mythical Pokémon. He became a member of Project Mew, a team selected to find it. For a brief moment, Mew even appeared in the palm of his hand!

Black sweatpants

GOH'S POKÉMON

Scorbunny

This Rabbit Pokémon has real fancy footwork! Full of energy, its Ember move involves racing around to create friction, then heating up a pebble to kick at an opponent. Moody in its Raboot phase, it evolves into the affectionate Cinderace.

KEY FACTS

Height:	1'
Weight:	9.9 lb
Type:	Fire
Category:	Rabbit
Weakness:	Water, Ground, and Rock

Fiery orange and yellow ears

Bandage over nose

BUNNY BUSINESS

Scorbunny was discovered living on the streets of Wyndon. It stole Ash's bag, with tasty scones inside, as it was feeding some hungry Nickit. It quickly bonded with Goh and was his first catch.

Orange toes

Grookey

A feisty and mischievous Chimp Pokémon, Grookey often spells trouble—but is also a great asset in a battle. When it drums out a beat with its stick, the sound brings energy and new life back to the tired Pokémon that hear it.

KEY FACTS

Height: 1'
Weight: 11 lb
Type: Grass
Category: Chimp
Weakness: Fire, Flying, Ice, Poison, and Bug

NO MONKEYING AROUND

When Chloe said Grookey was unreliable, it led to a challenge— could Grookey and Chloe's Eevee bring a simple delivery home? Despite taking a ride in the beak of Team Rocket's Pelipper, Grookey finally came through.

Stick can create a potent beat

Large pupils

Yellow markings around eyes

Curved tail

LEON

Famous throughout the world, Leon was unbeaten when he won the title of Monarch in the World Coronation Series. Known for his regal attire, he once took on and defeated a hundred contenders. Seemingly invincible, he lost his title to Ash in their recent final.

KEY FACTS

Height:	5' 7"
Weight:	116.8 lb
Type:	Steel-Ghost
Category:	Royal Sword
Weakness:	Fire, Ghost, Dark, and Ground

FRIENDLY FOE

Despite being Monarch, Leon has time for his young fan Ash at their first meeting. Amazingly, he agrees to a duel—fighting all out at Ash's request. When Leon wins, he gives Ash a Dynamax Band so he can grow his Pokémon to epic size.

Purple eye-like circle

Purple wing-shaped tips to arms

Aegislash

Leon is known for his sporting approach, as he compliments and encourages his rivals. Unpredictable, he varies his attacks and rarely repeats moves. He is an expert at Dynamax moves.

Crown design on cap brim

"To beat me, you've got a bit of work to do."

Plush red cloak

Regal gold trim

TAMING ETERNATUS

While he was training at Hammerlocke Gym, under Chairman Rose, Leon didn't realize he was being prepared for an encounter with the Legendary Pokémon, Eternatus. Leon helped trap Eternatus and later learned to harness its power.

LEON'S POKÉMON

Charizard

With moves such as Flamethrower, this Pokémon is always a red-hot contender in battle. Charizard can be hard to impress and often disobeys a new Trainer. However, once its respect is earned, it is deeply loyal.

KEY FACTS

Height: 5' 7"
Weight: 199.5 lb
Type: Fire-Flying
Category: Flame
Weakness: Water, Electric, and Rock

Fanged mouth

Powerful wings

Fiery end to tail

HOT STUFF

Charizard is a loyal ally that will accompany Leon on any adventure. It battled against a Gigantamaxed Centiskorch when Galar's Pokémon ran amok during the events leading to the Darkest Day.

Rillaboom

A powerful Pokémon with a deep connection to nature, Rillaboom can compete at the highest level, if well trained. Its drumming awakens the power of its special tree stump, enabling its roots to come to life and join it in battle.

KEY FACTS

Height:	6' 11"
Weight:	198.4 lb
Type:	Grass
Category:	Drummer
Weakness:	Fire, Flying, Ice, Poison, and Bug

BOOM AND BUST

This dynamic drummer plays a major role in the final battle between Leon and Ash. Using moves like Drum Beating, it pulverizes Ash's Dragonite and Sirfetch'd, but loses to the power of Dracovish.

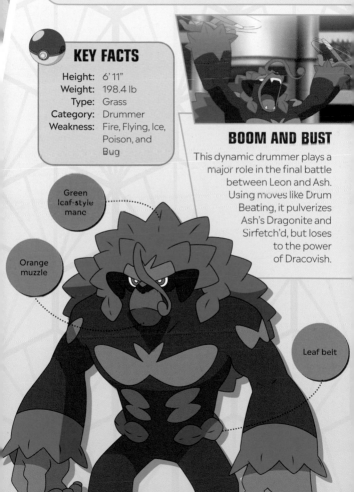

Green leaf-style mane

Orange muzzle

Leaf belt

CHALLENGE TIME!

Are you smart enough to be a Pokémon Master like Ash hopes to be? Battle the questions below, then turn over to see how you did!

1 **WHO'S THAT POKÉMON?**

Try and figure out these silhouettes!

2 **TRUE OR FALSE?**

a Ash's last name is Oak.

b Team Rocket's two most famous agents are Misty and Brock.

c If a Pokémon Dynamaxes, it means it grows to giant size.

3 CLOSE-UP CLUES

Can you pick out these Pokémon from their parts?

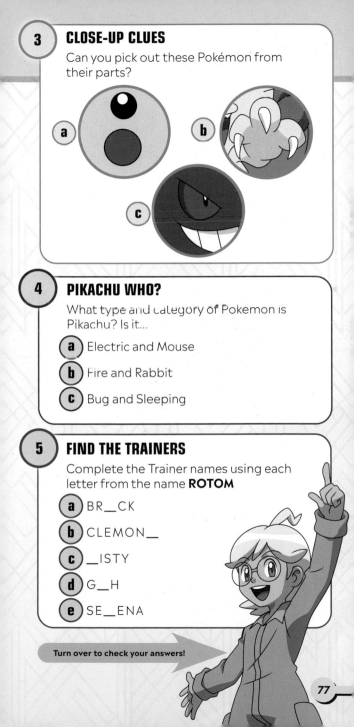

a

b

c

4 PIKACHU WHO?

What type and category of Pokémon is Pikachu? Is it...

a Electric and Mouse

b Fire and Rabbit

c Bug and Sleeping

5 FIND THE TRAINERS

Complete the Trainer names using each letter from the name **ROTOM**

a BR__CK

b CLEMON__

c __ISTY

d G__H

e SE__ENA

Turn over to check your answers!

ANSWERS

1 WHO'S THAT POKÉMON?

a Charizard

b Scorbunny

c Mew

2 TRUE OR FALSE?

a **False**—Ash's last name is Ketchum.

b **False**—Team Rocket's two most famous agents are Jessie and James.

c **True**—If a Pokémon Dynamaxes, it means it grows to giant size.

3 CLOSE-UP CLUES

a Pikachu

b Meowth

c Gengar

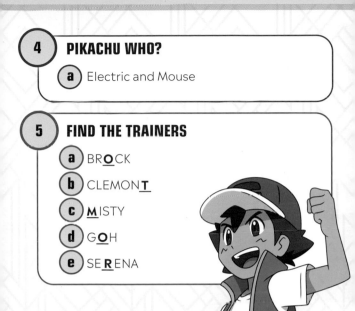

4 PIKACHU WHO?

a Electric and Mouse

5 FIND THE TRAINERS

a BR**O**CK

b CLEMON**T**

c **M**ISTY

d G**O**H

e SE**R**ENA

HOW DID YOU DO?

Now add up your score, giving yourself one point for each correct answer...

0-5 POINTS

Oops! Maybe Team Rocket sabotaged your answers! Try again!

6-10 POINTS

You're nearly as good as Ash. Why not learn more about Pokémon and have another go? It's a great excuse to read this book again!

11-15 POINTS

Congratulations! Like Ash, you might have what it takes to become a real Pokémon Master! Pikachu is proud of you.

Penguin Random House

Project Editor Lara Hutcheson
Designer Thelma-Jane Robb, James McKeag
Production Editor Siu Yin Chan
Senior Production Controller Lloyd Robertson
Managing Editor Paula Regan
Managing Art Editor Jo Connor
Publishing Director Mark Searle

First American Edition, 2024
Published in the United States by DK Publishing
1745 Broadway, 20th Floor, New York, NY 10019

Page design copyright © 2024 Dorling Kindersley Limited
DK, a Division of Penguin Random House LLC
24 25 26 27 28 10 9 8 7 6 5 4 3 2 1
001–339827–March/2024

A catalog record for this book
is available from the Library of Congress.
ISBN 978-0-7440-9470-1

DK books are available at special discounts when purchased
in bulk for sales promotions, premiums, fund-raising, or educational use.
For details, contact: DK Publishing Special Markets,
1745 Broadway, 20th Floor, New York, NY 10019
SpecialSales@dk.com

DK would like to thank Hank Woon and the rest of the team at The Pokémon
Company International. Thanks also to Jennette ElNagger for proofreading.

Printed and bound in China

www.dk.com
www.pokemon.com